As God Sees The Cross

As God Sees The Cross

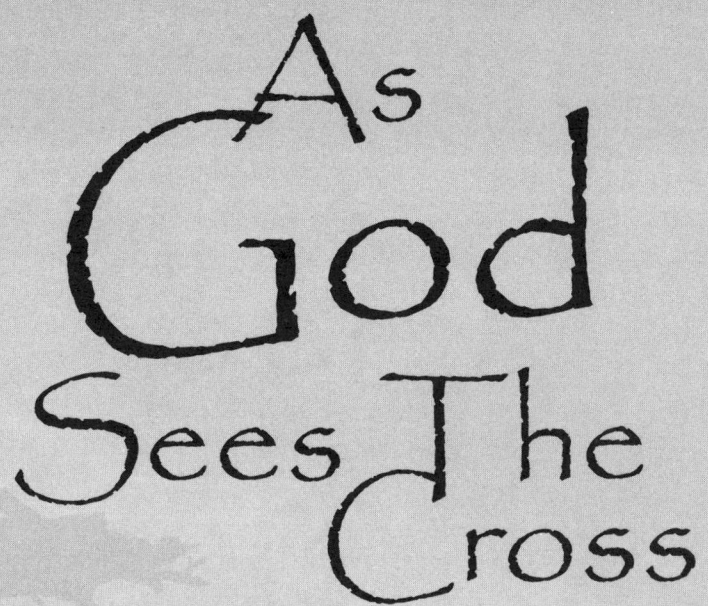

Barbara Markland

First printing © 2001
Second printing © 2004

Blessings Mailed Ministries
Post Office Box 1152
Midlothian, Virginia 23113

web site:
www.blessingsmailed.com

Cover design by David Jones, Richmond, VA
Photography by Trina Flannery, Richmond, VA

Scripture taken from the HOLY BIBLE, NEW INTERNATIONAL VERSION,
© 1973, 1978, 1984, International Bible Society.
Used by permission of Zondervan Bible Publishers.

James River Press, Richmond, VA

ISBN 0-9713070-5-9

The Bible tells the story of the cross.
God filled His Word with powerful details
meant to be understood.
Yet many of them are overlooked.
As we study God's Word, we begin to see the cross

A Word from the Author

There is a fresh hunger in people today to understand this treasure given to us by Almighty God ~ *known as The Bible*. I am honored to teach the Bible at women's retreats and conferences across the United States. For five years, it was my privilege to teach two weekly in-depth Bible studies. The heart of every Bible teacher loves to study and teach! When we share the Scriptures together at women's retreats, I am deeply moved by the expressions I see on their faces. Women of all ages, longing to understand the Bible, begin to see God's consistent patterns and marvelous word pictures. They realize the depth of the Father's saving love for them in the giving of His exquisite love gift ~ Jesus, the Son of God. *And their hearts respond with awe.*

As God Sees The Cross expresses the awe we experienced during a year-long study of Matthew's Gospel. We joined the disciples in their adventure following Jesus of Nazareth, and our journey was incredibly blessed. As we understood the Old Testament details fulfilled so completely in Jesus, the Lord took us to a deeper understanding of The Cross, *and grew in each of us a strong hunger for more.*

The Bible is God's love letter to us. When the hearts of men and women are exposed to His powerful, life-changing, eternal Word, our hearts cannot resist crying out for *more!* I pray that this Bible study will trigger your desire for *more*.

*With humility, in awe of God,
Who enabled me to write this Bible study
in eleven days.*

The Story of Israel

The Bible is a story, a love story between Almighty God and His children. The story begins with His sovereign creation of all things by His spoken Word. Psalm 33:9 states: "For He spoke and it came to be; He commanded and it stood firm." In the midst of His creation was a beautiful garden paradise. Almighty God then created man and woman in His image and allowed them to live in His garden paradise. In perfect love, the Lord desired that man and woman would live in harmony with Him. But it wasn't to be. His beloved creatures were quick to sin against their Creator, and painful consequences followed. Forced to leave their perfect garden paradise, the man and woman were condemned to death for their sin and began life outside the garden in a now imperfect, sinful world. But in His loving kindness, God promised a Messiah was coming who would die in place of His children, a Messiah was coming to save them.

As the man and woman bore children and nations began, the painful effects of sin were widespread. Almighty God chose one small nation from the mighty nations of the world and set it aside as His treasured possession. Through that nation, God would rescue His precious children from the consequences of sinning against their Creator. From the small nation of Israel, God promised deliverance for the peoples of all nations. Almighty God promised the world a Savior, His own Son.

And so, Israel was set aside as God's own, as a people committed to Jehovah God. They were commanded by God to follow His Law and remain holy, because one day the Son of God, the promised Messiah, would be born into the Jewish nation. Israel holds a very special place in the eyes of Almighty God, not because of her great size or strength, because she has neither. By God's sovereignty, He chose this small nation through which He would give all nations the gift of salvation.

God commanded Israel to live set apart and be watchful for the coming of the Promised Messiah. For centuries, through the voices of His chosen prophets, God foretold hundreds of clues surrounding the birth, life, death and resurrection of the coming Messiah. It was the desire of God's heart that the children of Israel would accept His great gift of grace, and would proclaim to the nations of the world that salvation is available through the Name of His Son. But instead, the children of Israel refused to recognize Jesus of Nazareth as the Son of God when He came, and instead, rejected and crucified their long-awaited Messiah. Had God's plan of salvation gone awry?

What happened in Jerusalem two thousand years ago?

The Story of the Cross

How much do you know about the last hours of Christ? So much emotion ... so much pain ... so much prophecy all swirled together in so few hours. The events of those hours continue to be *the* greatest drama in all history. The events of those hours affect the life of every person who will ever live. Do you wonder why Christ had to die *like that?* Have you ever questioned the significance of *His blood*? By studying the patterns in the Old Testament, we will view the cross from God's eyes ~~ seeing *"As God Sees The Cross."*

You will never see the cross the same way again.

The evening began with *The Intimate Supper* where Christ made an astonishing proposal to everyone who will accept. *The Secret Trials* took place under cover of darkness and were layered with irony. *The Public Execution* of Jesus of Nazareth by Roman crucifixion occurred outside the city gates of Jerusalem and devastated His followers. Then very early Sunday morning, *The Eternal Resurrection* rocked the world and changed everything *forever!*

So much happened in so few hours ~ the Old Covenant ended and the New Covenant began; a promise made before the foundation of the world was kept and Paradise was opened again! Jesus Christ proclaimed publicly that

He is the eternal Son of God risen from the dead!

The Bible clearly states that many people over a period of forty days saw Jesus *alive again* after His public death. He appeared to over 500 people at one time. [I Corin 15:6]

How much do you know about the cross?

You are about to study the most significant drama in all history. It is a story rich with interesting characters:

"A certain man" who offered Jesus his home
Judas, who betrayed Jesus
Peter, the friend who denied Jesus
Malchus, the servant
Pilate, the Governor of Judea
Herod, the self-proclaimed king of the Jews
Barabbas, the released murderer
Roman centurion, who stood at the cross
Joseph of Arimathea, who offered Jesus his tomb

But all characters pale in comparison with Jesus, who claimed to be the Son of God, the promised Messiah that the Jewish nation had long awaited. According to eyewitnesses like Peter and John, Jesus performed astounding miracles, fulfilling every prophecy written about the first coming of Messiah. According to secular historian Flavius Josephus, Jesus "appeared to them alive again after the third day, as the divine prophets had foretold these and ten thousand other wonderful things concerning him." *

Is it all true? And what does it mean to you?
It means *everything*.

If Jesus of Nazareth is the promised Messiah,
He came to die.
If Jesus of Nazareth is the Son of God,
He came to die so you can live.

The last hours of Christ are the crowning jewel of history.
This is His story.

CONTENTS

The Intimate Supper

Preparing for Passover	17
Many Making Plans	23
An Intimate Proposal	27
The Cup of Salvation	32

The Secret Trials

Fickle Vow, Faithful Vow	39
Unwelcome Garden Guests	44
Forsaking Law and Lord	49
No Fault Found in Him	53

The Public Execution

The Promise of the Cross	61
Walking the Blood Path	67
The Daily Sacrifice	72
The Cries from the Cross	78

The Eternal Resurrection

The Earth Shook	87
A Sign in a Secure Tomb	92
Atonement	99
Powerful Evidence	106

Leader's Guide 117

The Intimate Supper

Preparing for Passover

Did you know a Jewish celebration was underway on the night we commonly call The Last Supper? We begin by reading **Mark 14:12.** According to the Bible, what were they celebrating?

The Jews ate the Passover meal on this night. Very special preparations had to be made for this meal. Understanding the significance of the Passover makes these events come alive, so let's do a little Old Testament investigating.

The Exodus of the Jewish people from slavery in Egypt to freedom in the wilderness is one of the greatest miracles of God's rescue of His people. The second book of the Bible, the Book of Exodus, tells the fascinating story of deliverance.

Exodus means deliverance!

Maybe you know the story ~ God sent ten nasty plagues on Pharaoh and all of Egypt; Moses boldly told Pharaoh that God said, "Let My people go!" and finally they did go! God parted the Red Sea and over two million people walked right through on dry ground!

That's worth celebrating, isn't it?
But there's more ...

What Jesus and His disciples were celebrating that night was actually a remembrance of the 10th plague. Please look at **Exodus 11:4-7.**

That was a truly horrible night in Egypt. But God said He would do something special regarding Israel. What was it?

God had given instructions to be carried out by the people of Israel ahead of time so they were ready for that night. Please read **Exodus 12:1-5**. God changed their calendar and said this month is the beginning of your *Happy New Year!* On the 10th day of this month, what were they to do?

This day came to be known as **Lamb Selection Day**. Remember that; it plays a wonderful part in this drama! On the 14th day important events happened! **Exodus 12:6-8** gives God's **very specific** instructions. List them below.

We will soon see why it was crucial that they obeyed God's instructions *to the letter.* God was protecting His people from unseen dangers ahead. He will do that today if we follow His instructions for our lives.

How wise we are when we obey!

The LORD is about to make the distinction between Egypt and Israel. Any ideas what it might be? Read **Exodus 12:12-13** to find out. Why do you think the Jews call this holiday *Passover*?

What a powerful visual! God said paint the doorposts to your home ~ the entrance to your very life ~ with innocent blood. When the plague of death came, God promised to ***pass over*** and spare everyone covered by innocent blood.

Read God's instruction in **Exodus 12:24-28**. What were they to do?

God spared His people from death on that miraculous Passover night. He instituted a wonderful week-long festival, the *Feast of Unleavened Bread*, so they would **remember**. He said teach the children that their God is mighty indeed!

Have you taught your children this wonderful truth?

That night all the people of Israel made their *exodus* out of Egypt. They were delivered from bondage to freedom!

Read **Exodus 12:40-41**. How long were they enslaved in Egypt and what detail do you notice in God's Word?

God is a God of details. *Remember that.* There are incredible details in the events of the last hours of Christ.

Soon we will join Jesus and His disciples and see the meaning of the Passover meal come alive. Before we do, something happened earlier that last week that is too powerful to miss. Look at **John 12:1-6.** Jesus is in Bethany with close friends, Lazarus, Martha and Mary. According to John, how many days until Passover?

Write down everything we learn about Judas from this meal that is commonly thought to have occurred on Saturday night, six days prior to the cross.

Look at **John 12:12-13,** describing the next day, the Sunday before the cross. How many days now until Passover?

Passover began sundown Thursday and ended sundown Friday. Remember: God told Israel to choose their Passover lamb on the 10th day and slaughter their Passover lamb on the 14th day. To determine the exact day **John 12:12** is referring to, count backward beginning with Thursday, which was Passover, and be sure to count Thursday. Do you remember any significance to this day from Exodus 12:3?

The day Jesus chose to make His Triumphal Entry into Jerusalem was a most special day. It is recorded in all four gospels ~ Matthew 21, Mark 11, Luke 19 and John 12. Counting backward from Thursday, the 14th day, we discover that Jesus rode into Jerusalem on the 10th day of the month, known to all the Jewish people as

Lamb Selection Day.

On the day God instructed every Jewish family to choose their Passover lamb, *God's Passover Lamb, His own Son,* rode triumphantly into Jerusalem on a donkey, offering Himself for the sin of the world and fulfilling Scripture. [**Matthew 21:6-11.**]

God chose **that very day** to present His Son and ask:

*" Here is My Passover Lamb;
will you choose Him?"*

By examining details, we will see the Bible is not a book of simple stories. It is a *meticulous* account of God's compassion and love for His people. It is a *mighty* account of God's promise to send a Messiah to deliver His people from death, to bring *exodus* to us! It is a *miraculous* account of the life-changing events when Messiah died to save His people, then rose to life again.

*God's Word is the story of Jesus,
the Lamb of God.*

God is still asking that question ~ *will you choose Him?*

Make a list for yourself in the space below of everything you have learned so far. Details are very important in the last hours of Christ.

Many Making Plans

Jesus was a Jewish rabbi. He was required to observe all Jewish holidays with His disciples, especially the Passover. The disciples of Jesus made preparations for the Passover meal exactly as He told them. Read **Matthew 26:17-19**.

The disciples were not the only ones busy making preparations. The Pharisees and chief priests of Israel were busy plotting to arrest Jesus "in some sly way" and kill Him, but they didn't want to do it during Passover because they were afraid of the people. [**Matthew 26:3-5**] People were so drawn to Jesus that the Pharisees couldn't get near Him for the crowds! They were torn between their fear of arousing the crowds and their intense hatred for Jesus. They needed a solution ...

The sad irony is the solution came to them, walking right into their evil midst. Read **Matthew 26:14-16**. Who offers to betray Jesus and what is the price of betrayal?

How do you think the chief priests and Pharisees responded to Judas' offer of betrayal? See **Mark 14:10-11**.

The infamous thirty pieces of silver was not a great deal of money. It may surprise you to learn what role this detail plays in the drama. Write what we learn about thirty pieces of silver from **Exodus 21:32**.

Jesus was willing to be betrayed for the price of a slave ~ thirty pieces of silver.

Why do you think Judas betrayed Jesus?

Take a moment to read **Philippians 2:5-11.** This beautiful scripture tells us that Jesus, the Son of God, made Himself *nothing!* What nature did He take on? [see **verse 7**]

Servant is another name for *slave*.
What does that tell you about Jesus?

While the chief priests and Pharisees were making plans to kill Him, and Judas watched for an opportunity to hand Him over "when no crowd was present," [**Luke 22:6**] Jesus had already made plans of His own. He would soon eat His last Passover meal with His disciples ~ a meal that would be the *most important meal in history*. Read again **Matthew 26:18** and record what role a "certain man" plays in the events.

Isn't that just like Jesus ... He asked a very simple request of that "certain man" and then *blessed* him by hosting the most important meal in all history in his home!

That's also a testimony of the loyal love of Jesus. If you recall a time when Jesus asked you for what seemed like such a small thing and then blessed you for it, write it down so you remember. Share your story if you can. You may be just the encouragement someone else needs to say *yes* to Jesus!

Our LORD speaks to us through His Word when we study. Have you recently felt the need to call someone you haven't spoken to in years or write a long-overdue note? These are some of the ways Jesus asks us to do something for Him, and then blesses the results. Have you been reluctant to answer *yes* to Jesus? In light of what you've learned from the "certain man," what should you do and why?

So many were busy making plans! The chief priests and Pharisees secretly plotted to kill Jesus without arousing the people. Their hatred of Jesus was only exceeded by their frustration at their inability to make their plan happen! Then along came Judas, seeking to line his pockets with thirty pieces of silver for betraying his Master. No wonder they were *delighted* ... now it was just a matter of time.

Does it seem like the "bad guys" are winning and the plans are all *wrong*? Read very carefully **Isaiah 46:9-10.** How should we view these events from God's perspective?

Time is indeed running out. The cross is only hours away. How does Jesus spend those last hours? First He will share *The Intimate Supper* with His disciples. Now that we have learned what Passover means, watch the Old Testament teachings come to life and take on new meaning. During this intimate meal with His disciples, Jesus lifted the cup and made a profound statement.

Continue your list of all you've learned in this lesson.

Remember Who is in charge!

An Intimate Proposal

Jesus and His disciples sharing a meal together ~ by now it was a familiar practice. They'd broken bread together many times and enjoyed several Passover celebrations. But this was their last supper together before the cross.

Jesus alone knew the agony of this long night.

Jesus served as Passover host to His disciples. The Passover meal consisted of unleavened bread, bitter herbs and an assortment of foods symbolic of God's miraculous *exodus* of His people from Egypt. There were four cups of wine at different intervals throughout the Passover meal. At the third cup, *the cup of salvation*, Jesus changed everything.

As everyone settled in and got comfortable, Jesus got up. Read **John 13:2-11**. What did Jesus do and what was Peter's response?

How would you have responded if you had been there?

Write down everything the Bible teaches us about Jesus from this passage.

Read **John 13:7** again. Why do you think Jesus said that?

Hard to imagine, isn't it, that Jesus knelt before each of His disciples ~ including Judas ~ and washed their feet. Read words Jesus had spoken earlier to His disciples in **Matthew 20:25-28.** List all the ways you have seen the word "servant" associated with Jesus.

After He finished this marvelous display of humble s*ervanthood*, Jesus followed it up with important teaching. Read **John 13:14-17.** As you "see" Jesus washing feet and setting an example for us to follow, are there any changes Jesus wants to make in your attitude?

The songs sung during the Passover celebration were traditionally **Psalms 113-118**. Jesus, the Son of God, sang these Scriptures aloud to His Father.

It is deeply moving to realize **Jesus knew** that the words He sang aloud were painfully prophetic of **what was to come.** Read **Psalm 116:3-4.** "*Hosanna*" means "Save me." When had the people cried "*Hosanna*" to Jesus earlier that week?

See **Psalm 116:12-13**. Any thoughts as to when Jesus will "lift up" the *cup of salvation*?

Revelation 13:8 describes Jesus as the "Lamb that was slain from the creation of the world." That verse confirms that before the foundation of the world, Jesus knew that we would sin against Him and need a Savior. Knowing our need, the Son made a vow to the Father that Jesus would be our Passover Lamb and willingly die in our place.

Jesus *always knew* that He would face the agony of crucifixion for us. It's staggering to think about it, isn't it? Read the Scripture Jesus sang aloud in **Psalm 116:14**. Write any new significance you see in these words.

There are two other verses Jesus sang aloud that we must read. Write **Psalm 118:6**. We'll come back to this later.

Lastly, read **Psalm 118:25-26**. If you remembered those words from His Triumphal Entry into Jerusalem just days earlier on Lamb Selection Day, you were right! [see **Matthew 21:8-9**] What do you think those same voices who cried "Hosanna" will be screaming about Jesus in just a few hours?

Jesus celebrated two memorial meals with His disciples in the home of a "certain man" that evening. It was at the first meal, the traditional Passover, that Jesus startled everyone. Write His words from **Matthew 26:21.**

Imagine Judas' reaction! He thought he was so clever and so careful! He was sure Jesus would never know ... but when we read **Matthew 9:4, Matthew 12:25** and **Luke 11:17**, what do we learn about Jesus?

Peter responded just like we would ... *he wanted to know who!* He motioned to the disciple John to ask Jesus: "Lord, who is it?" **[John 13:25]** Read how Jesus responded in **John 13:26.** Do you think Jesus set Judas up? Why or why not?

What do you think Judas saw when he looked into the eyes of Jesus that night? What did Jesus see in Judas?

In the culture of that day, the seat next to the host was the seat of honor. Jesus placed Judas at His side in the seat of honor during the meal. It was also an honor for the Host of the Passover to offer a guest bread for dipping. In two ways we see Jesus honored Judas.

*Knowing Judas was His betrayer,
Jesus placed him in the seat of honor.*

The results of bad choices are usually painful and often permanent. **John 13:30** tells us that "As soon as Judas had taken the bread, he went out. And *it was night.*" Judas left the very presence of the Son of God to go out into the darkness ... *spiritual as well as physical darkness.*

What do we learn from Judas about our choices?

What do we learn about Jesus?

As Judas went out into the darkness, the traditional Passover meal changed. The special part of the evening which followed was celebrated only by the ones who truly loved Jesus. With them, He would share profound words and demonstrate the true meaning of the *cup of salvation*.

Continue compiling the significant details you've noticed.

The Cup of Salvation

To understand the second part of the evening ~ the special meal that took place after Judas left ~ we need to understand Middle Eastern customs regarding marriage. They are very different than ours. In the time of Jesus, betrothal negotiations took place between the fathers of the bridegroom and the bride. They weren't discussing caterers! They haggled over what was known as *The Bride Price ~ the price the bridegroom was willing to pay for his bride.* This price was costly indeed, comparable to a new home today.

After *The Bride Price was agreed,* the bridegroom's father poured a cup of wine and gave it to his son. The bridegroom then stood in front of the bride, offered her the cup and said:
   "This cup I offer to you. I love you. I offer you my life."

Now the young woman must decide. She would either say, "No, I don't want your life." Or she would take the cup and drink. By drinking the cup, she affirmed to the bridegroom:
   "I accept your life and give you mine in return."

When the intimate Passover supper between Jesus and His disciples reached the 3rd cup of wine, the **Cup of Salvation**, Jesus changed the traditional wording. He raised the cup of salvation, gave thanks to His Father, offered it to His disciples ~ and us ~ and in effect He said:

"This cup I offer to you.
I love you. I offer you My life.
Will you be My spiritual bride?"

See **Matthew 26:27-28**. Who is invited to drink the cup?

*The Bridegroom offers Himself
to everyone who will accept His proposal.*

God, the Father of the Bridegroom, sent His Son to earth
to purchase a bride for Himself. That bride is His Church.

God, the Father of the Bride, set *The Bride Price* to pay,
and it was a staggering price.
*Deliver them from sin and death with your blood.
Offer yourself as Passover Lamb for them.*

What Christ did on the cross provided the *eternal exodus* for His Church. When we cover the entrance to our life ~ the door of our heart ~ with the innocent blood of Jesus, we are delivered from eternal death. God promises to accept the blood of Jesus as our innocent Lamb. Though we deserve to die for our sin, yet we live.

In the midst of a night of betrayal, sorrow and untold agony
~ all caused by our sinfulness ~
we are invited into a Sacred Romance with Jesus.

It is for this purpose that He came,
to give His life for His Bride,   His Church,
for all who will accept the gift of His life.

Jesus is our Bridegroom.

As you contemplate that *you* are the spiritual bride of Christ, what new significance will the Lord's Supper have for you?

Each time you celebrate the Lord's Supper, you are affirming that "I am the Spiritual Bride of Christ!" Look back with gratitude and remember the costly *Bride Price* that Jesus paid for your life. Look forward with anticipation and remember your Bridegroom is coming back! Until He does, promise Him you will remain spiritually pure and faithful to Him alone.

Think carefully about the ways you allow the world to make you spiritually impure. Make a list of anything that comes before Jesus in your heart and causes you to be unfaithful to Him.

Jesus spoke incredible words to His disciples that evening. After His proposal of spiritual marriage, He comforted them and prepared them for what would soon take place. As you read **John 13:31-16:33**, keep in mind the timing. When He left this room, Jesus was soon arrested and crucified. Record some thoughts about the teaching Jesus chose to share with them just before the cross.

Read his prayer in **John 17:1-26.**   Who did Jesus pray for in those moments as The Intimate Supper ended?

Jesus was praying for you. In those beautiful words, He prayed for Himself, for His disciples, and for you. Jesus prayed for everyone who will believe in Him.

The Passover feast ended with singing **Psalm 136.** It's the perfect song, a marvelous retelling of Israel's Exodus from Egypt! Psalm 136 is a responsive psalm. It is likely Jesus sang the first line and the disciples sang the responsive line: "*His love endures forever.*"   Truly, it does.

Look back again to **Psalm 118:6.** Remember that Jesus sang those words earlier in the evening.   *What can man do to Him*? You'll be horrified to see what we did to Him. **All of us.** The Lamb of God came to take away the sin of the world — **ours**.

The Intimate Supper has come to an end.   It has been a Passover meal like none other for the disciples.   There is an energy in the air that is unsettling as they leave the room and begin the short walk to the Mount of Olives. Their destination is a very familiar place ~ the beautiful garden known as Gethsemane, the *"Olive Press"* ~ where Jesus frequently spent time in prayer with His Father.   But on this fateful night the garden's tranquility will be disturbed by:

> the plea of the Son who obeys,
> the kiss of the enemy who betrays,
> the sword of the friend who disowns.

He prayed for you to believe in Him.

Continue compiling your list of details, ironies and lessons learned thus far as you study.

The Secret Trials

Fickle Vow, Faithful Vow

As Jesus and His disciples traveled the familiar path back to the Mount of Olives, the night became a personal nightmare for Peter. After announcing one of the Twelve would betray Him, Jesus shocked the group again by declaring "this very night you will all fall away on account of Me." **[Matthew 26:31]** Stunned by His declaration, they didn't listen when Jesus prophesied that "After I have **risen**, I will go ahead of you into Galilee." **[Matthew 26:32]**

Read Peter's response to Jesus in **Matthew 26:33.** What is Peter's state of mind about his ability to remain faithful to Jesus, as compared to the other disciples?

Jesus warned Peter of his upcoming denial. Peter vowed he would die with Jesus but never disown Him! We know that, sadly, Peter disowned Christ three times. Based on his exchange with Jesus, how should Peter have responded?

When they arrive at Gethsemane, Jesus asks Peter, James and John to keep watch with Him. **[Matthew 26:36-38]**
How does Jesus describe what He is feeling, and what do you think is happening to Him?

That Passover night Jesus asked His three closest disciples to: *be my friend; stay with me; pray with me* in the darkest hour of my life. It was the only time Jesus ever asked anything for Himself. Peter vowed to die for Jesus, but couldn't keep his vow. What *did* Peter do? See **Matthew 26:40.**

According to Jesus, what should Peter have been doing? **See Matthew 26:41.**

How could the advice Jesus gave Peter help us in our trials?

Jesus knew He would face His agony in the Garden of Gethsemane alone. Jesus made a vow to die *because* man is weak against sin ... why would He expect man to be strong now? As the Son of God, He *knew* what must be done. And as the Son of Man, He *dreaded* it.

Jesus would face three kinds of suffering ~ physical, emotional and spiritual. Which of the three do you think would be the worst to endure and why?

The physical suffering ~ the Roman cross was so intense, a new word was coined to describe it: *excruciating*. The root word "*cross*" is the heart of this word describing agony.

The emotional suffering ~ knowing the contemptible plan to arrest and kill Him by the ones He vowed to die for; they would mock & humiliate Him, spit on Him & refuse to believe.

The spiritual suffering ~ knowing the Father would pour out on the Son all His wrath against the sinful, ugly, selfish filth of man's ways.

Jesus knew He would face it alone.

And so in the Garden, *alone,* Jesus fell to the ground and suffered the mental agony of what was to come. His friends slept while He wept. What does **Matthew 26:39** tell us Jesus did, and what did He ask?

What "cup" do you think He is referring to?

Read **Matthew 26:39** and **Matthew 26:42.** What change do you see take place in the way Jesus prays to His Father?

Jesus begged God to change His mind. God responded by saying, "No," and Jesus accepted the answer. Write His *five powerful words of victory.*

How many times did Jesus pray? [**Matthew 26:44**] What can we learn from His example?

Suppose His Father had taken away the "cup" from Jesus; what do you think would be the consequence for you?

God knew what Jesus would endure by drinking the "cup." Every horrible detail, every torturous pain, every mocking word, every stripe from the flogging, every drop of blood that Jesus would shed, *God knew it.* But God also knew there was no other way His purpose ~ *to save us from death* ~ could be accomplished except through the death of Jesus. Maybe you're facing a trial, an illness or a painful situation right now. God may not choose to take your "cup" away either, but you can know that God *will* give you the strength to get through it so His purpose can be accomplished.

What purpose might God want to accomplish by our trials?

Trials in our life bring us to the realization that we must depend on God. Our faith grows when we discover how much we can trust our Father. *He always proves faithful.*

Jesus lay down in that Garden weak, but *stood up strong.*
What was the source of His strength?

Do you think that same strength is available to you? How could that make a difference in the next trial in your life?

Filled with strength from God, Jesus was able to stand up and "fulfill His vow to the LORD in the presence of all the people." Hear Him say *victoriously,* "The hour is near, and the Son of Man is betrayed into the hands of sinners. Rise, let us go! Here comes My betrayer." **[Matthew 26:45-46]**

Continue your journal as you learn from God's Word.

Jesus was alone, but we are never alone.

Unwelcome Garden Guests

The bright glow of lanterns lit up the sky as the sound of many feet approached the Garden. Having just awakened from sleep, the disciples were slow to grasp what was happening. Are you frustrated with them, wondering why they couldn't stay awake and *be there* for Jesus when He needed friends??? **Luke 22:45** may provide a clue. What condition were they in when Jesus woke them?

List reasons why the disciples would be feeling that way.

His "appointed time" [**Matthew 26:18**] arrived when the unwelcome guests entered the Garden. Read **John 18:2-4**. Bible scholars place the number of soldiers in this detachment between 300-500, as well as "some officials from the chief priests and Pharisees." What had they agreed on earlier with Judas? Read **Luke 22:6.**

What irony do you see in this?

Why did Judas lead them to Gethsemane to find Jesus?

Write the fact about Jesus that **John 18:4** reiterates for us.

The Bible is clear: Jesus was *completely aware* of what would happen, *completely willing* to allow it to happen, and *completely in control* of the events as they happened.

Jesus even initiated the confrontation! What does He ask?

Read **John 18:5-9.** This detachment contains hundreds of the most highly trained soldiers. What happened?

Again, because the Old Testament is the key to understanding what happened in the New Testament, we will go back to Exodus. God called to Moses on Mt. Sinai, saying: "So now, go. I am sending you to Pharaoh to bring my people the Israelites out of Egypt." **[Exodus 3:10]**

Pretty incredible marching orders! Moses had one question of the One the Israelites knew only as "the God of Abraham, Isaac and Jacob" ~~ "What is Your *Name*?" [**v. 13**]

> God revealed His *Name* to Moses:
> " I AM WHO I AM. " [**v.14**]

That *Name* was sufficient for an enslaved people to march out of bondage, become a nation and birth a Savior! They learned the Power of the Almighty is His Name **"I AM."**

And now years later in the Garden of Gethsemane, this "select crowd" would learn the Power of that *Name*!

This "select crowd" came asking for Jesus of Nazareth and Jesus complied with their request. He introduced them to **Jesus of Nazareth**! The Greek word Jesus used in His response to them literally translates **"I AM."** For that brief incredible moment, the Son of God unveiled His glory and allowed them a glimpse of Majesty.

Several hundred highly trained, highly skilled fighting soldiers *fell backward to the ground like dominos*! Why?

What a humiliating scene it was! As they composed themselves, Jesus *again asks them:* "Who is it you want?"

He still asks the same question:

Do you want the world or Me?
Who is it you want?

Normally the followers would be arrested with the leader. Why do you think this happened differently? [**John 18:8-9**]

As can be expected, impetuous Peter reacted when the soldiers came for *his* Jesus! Read **John 18:10-11**. What did Peter do and how did Jesus respond?

In the midst of this madness in the Garden, the servant Malchus is wounded, Judas is betraying Jesus with a hypocritical kiss, the Jewish officials are sneering at Him in gloating victory, and hundreds of soldiers are preparing to arrest Him.

Luke 22:50-51 records the *wonder* of Jesus. What did He do? How do you respond to that?

Read **Matthew 26:52-54.** Why will Jesus not allow His Father to put 72,000 angels at His disposal?

Hundreds of soldiers came to arrest Jesus.
Millions of soldiers wouldn't have been enough
unless He was willing.

For our sake Jesus was w*illing* to present Himself on Lamb Selection Day, *willing* to place His betrayer, Judas in the seat of honor, *willing* to heal the ear of one who came after Him with a mob, *willing* to place Himself in the hands of those who should fall at His feet. *He was willing* to endure it all for *us*.

Jesus would endure a grueling night of secret trials and public accusations. In the morning the Son of God would be condemned to die for the sin of the world.

He knew what was coming, and He was willing.

Continue your list of details and irony. Include everything you are now seeing from a new perspective.

Forsaking Law and Lord

Did you know Jesus endured *six* trials during that grueling night? Three religious trials followed by three political trials, or call it three Jewish trials followed by three Gentile trials. In other words, *everyone* was guilty in this shameful display.

It was a night of contrasts. By the time morning arrived, the Jewish leaders would break every rule they meticulously governed themselves by in order to crucify Jesus during Passover, *the exact time they did not want to*! [please see **Matthew 26:4-5** ~ the "Feast" means the Passover.]

Jesus was first taken to the home of Annas, the former high priest of Israel. Even though his son-in-law Caiphas was currently high priest, Annas still held much power in the eyes of the Jewish people. It was there that Annas and some of the official governing body of the Jews, the Sanhedrin, conducted an informal inquiry of Jesus, trial #1. The cruelty began immediately.

Read **John 18:19-24** [the "high priest" refers to Annas.] What happened?

Still bound, Jesus was then taken to the home of Caiphas. What began as an irregular trial soon turned into a mob scene. The teachers of the law and elders of Israel began arriving about 3:00 a.m. ~ leaving their beds in the middle of the night! What could be so important? *Getting rid of Jesus!*

Trial #2, the irregular trial, occurred as members continued gathering. Then approximately 5:00 a.m. *official* trial #3 began when a quorum of the Sanhedrin had arrived.

The Sanhedrin could be compared to our Supreme Court.
This was the religious and political authority of Israel with the high priest presiding. A quick look at the rules of the Sanhedrin will show the hypocrisy of this night.

> All criminal cases must be completed in the daytime.
> All evidence of innocence is presented *first*.
> Everything must be corroborated by two witnesses;
>   witnesses never have contact with each other.
> When a guilty verdict is reached, a night must elapse
>   before sentencing so mercy feelings can develop.
> No decision is valid unless conducted in their
>   official meeting place, the *Hall of Hewn Stone*.
> No official meetings conducted on the morning of a
>   feast day.

Read **Mark 14:53-59**. Compile an evidence list of every instance in which the Sanhedrin did not abide by their rules.

How do you think Jesus felt, wrists bound, *watching*, as the Jewish leaders frantically tried to agree on false testimony to convict the Son of God?

They weren't interested in fairness or justice. **They refused to accept Jesus as their Messiah and wanted him dead**. First they needed a charge against Him. Thus far Jesus had watched in silence; Caiphas would force Jesus to respond. Read **Matthew 26:62-63**. Write the charge under oath.

To understand why the charge under oath forced Jesus to answer, read **Leviticus 5:1** in the Old Testament. What must Jesus do to remain sinless?

If Jesus answers "No," they have won, the crisis is over and everyone can go back to bed. If Jesus answers "Yes," what do you think He will be accused of?

What do you suppose Satan was whispering in His ear in that moment before Jesus answered?

"Tell us if you are the Christ, the Son of God."

How grateful we are that Jesus said, *"Yes, it is as you say."* **[Matthew 26:64]** Our Passover Lamb remained perfect!

Something very significant happened next. Please read **Matthew 26:64-66**. What did the high priest do?

Is this detail significant? *Every Biblical detail is significant!* God had specific rules the high priest must follow in order to serve in God's house, the temple. **Leviticus 21:10** tells something the high priest *must not do*. What is it?

Alert!! Israel's high priest is no longer fit to serve. But the daily sacrifice must be offered on this day as every other day. Remember that; it will be a significant detail later.

Finally in **Matthew 26:65** they agree on the charge against Jesus. What is it and do you see any irony in that?

Read what might be one of the saddest verses in the Bible, **Mark 14:64-65.** The first vicious beating of Jesus comes at the hand of the Jews. This is one of many fulfilled prophecies [**Isaiah 50:6**]. They played a nasty game known as "Hot Hand" in which they blindfolded the victim, slapped him and made him guess who hit him. An incorrect guess resulted in another slap. What is foolish about playing "Hot Hand" with a blindfolded Jesus?

His enemies spit on Him, slapped Him and pulled out His beard. His friend out in the courtyard disowned Him three times. Jesus stood alone, enduring humiliation, disgrace and violence. And the worst is yet to come.

"He is worthy of death."

What struck you the most about the first three trials?

As you continue your journal, list every example of hypocrisy that night.

No Fault Found in Him

The Roman court opened at sunrise, 6:00 a.m. Roman time. It was common knowledge that Pilate refused additional cases after the docket filled. Sometime near 6:00 a.m. when the Jewish leaders finally arrived at their charge of *Blasphemy,* a courier was quickly dispatched to alert Pilate they were bringing Jesus before him. The religious leaders of Israel placed Jesus, who claimed to be their long-awaited Messiah, into the hands of the cruel, hated Roman empire.

Pontius Pilate, Governor of Judea, had gotten off to a bad start with the Jews. He was intolerant of their religion and their constant squabbling; and weary of their feast days that invariably led to trouble. There is good reason to believe Pilate had recently been chastised by Caesar because of his inability to control the Jews; job security may be an issue!

Here they come, bright and early at 6:00 a.m., bringing their latest religious squabble into his court. Well, actually not *into* his court. Their hypocrisy won't allow that. Please look at **John 18:28-31**. Why won't they enter the Gentile palace?

Read **Luke 23:1-2** to see the three charges against Jesus. *What happened to blasphemy???* Why do you think the Jews do not bring the charge of blasphemy before Pilate?

Claiming to be king was a direct threat to Rome. The Jews knew that charge would catch Pilate's attention! Pilate asked Jesus "the question of questions." See **Luke 23:3**. What did Pilate ask and how did Jesus answer him?

Why do you think Jesus chose to answer?

There is much emphasis on the *"you"* in Pilate's question, as if he's sarcastically asking, *"Are **you** the king of the Jews? You're beat-up and half dead; you've got to be kidding me."*

It doesn't take Pilate long to render his decision. His words will haunt him forever. Write them below. [**Luke 23:4**]

Pilate learned from the Jewish leaders that Jesus came from Galilee ~ which placed Him under Herod's authority and out of Pilate's hair! [**Luke 23:5-7**] Trial #4 is over in a hurry. Herod happened to be in Jerusalem over the Jewish Passover, and was quite anxious to see this Jesus he'd heard so much about. Herod hoped to be entertained by a miracle. Read **Luke 23:8-11** to see if Herod got his miracle. Describe the scene that took place in this trial #5.

Don't miss a significant detail noted in **Luke 23:12**.

Trial #6 is the one we're all most familiar with. As you read the four gospels, you get a sense that Pilate was amazed by how different Jesus was from the common criminal usually brought before Pilate. He saw no fear in Jesus' eyes; rather, a composed courage. Pilate may have wondered:

Who is judging whom?

Do you think Pilate's loathing for the Jewish leaders may have intensified as their vehement accusations were met with grace and dignity by Jesus? In an effort to appease the Jews, Pilate has Jesus cruelly flogged by Roman experts.

Note **John 19:1-3**. The second vicious beating Jesus suffered comes at the hands of the Gentiles. Jesus is then brought back outside wearing the crown of thorns and purple robe. To Pilate's dismay, even though Jesus is beaten beyond recognition at this point [**Isaiah 53:3**], the Jewish leaders will settle for nothing less than crucifixion.

How can Pilate get the matter out of his court? Perhaps they will accept a trade ~ Barabbas for Jesus. There is an interesting irony in this trade. According to Syrian writings at the time of Jesus, the full name of the convicted felon offered as a trade was *Jesus Barabbas*. This might explain why Pilate continually said "Jesus who is called Christ," as if to differentiate between the two. What does Barabbas mean? Bar means "son of" and Abba means "father."

Barabbas means "son of fathers."

Jesus earlier warned the Jewish people not to call anyone Father except God because the people called these hypocritical religious leaders "the Fathers." [**Matthew 23:9**] Standing before the Jewish people were two choices:

Jesus Barabbas, "son of the fathers,"
convicted felon,
"son" of the religious leaders of Israel

or

Jesus, "who is called Christ,"
innocent and sinless,
Son of *the Father* in heaven.

The people chose to follow their religious leaders rather than Jesus, and chose to cry for Barabbas instead of Jesus.

Note **John 19:6-7**. Discover whose voices are the first to cry out, "Crucify Him!" Are you surprised? When Pilate seems determined to release Jesus, the Jewish leaders play their *trump card.* See **John 19:12**. Why do you think this threat was effective?

Pilate gave in to their demands and "surrendered Jesus to their will." [**Luke 23:23-25**] He publicly washed his hands, but would never remove the stain of Jesus' blood. Roman law required capital punishment to be carried out immediately. Jesus would be crucified on Passover, exactly the time the Jewish leaders did not want ... *exactly the time God planned.*

Here is a sampling of the irony surrounding the trials:

The Jewish leaders ~
    prided themselves on keeping the Law,
        but broke every law that stood in the way of killing Jesus.
    deliberately started a riot in Pilate's court
        which they wanted to avoid [**Matthew 26:5**] to force Pilate to act.
    hated Caesar yet claimed Caesar as their king
        [**John 19:15**]; rejected their true King.
    forced Rome to crucify a Jewish citizen when
        Rome would never crucify a Roman citizen; crucifixion was for *slaves* and criminals.

Pilate ~
    had 3 chances to choose Jesus; instead chose to
        wash his hands, keep his job, please a mob.
    claimed in vain his innocence of Christ's blood;
        famous for his guilt with the infamous words "crucified under Pontius Pilate."

Peter -
    had 3 chances to pray; instead slept 3 times,
        then disowned his Lord 3 times.

Jesus -
    the "Good Shepherd" struck on the head with a staff
        by the "sheep" He would lay down His life for.
    the "Suffering Servant"
        betrayed for the price of a servant.
    the "Innocent Lamb"
        crucified in the manner of a criminal.

Nothing about this scenario makes sense to us. That's because, just like Peter, we "do not have in mind the things of God, but the things of men." **[Matthew 16:23]**

From our perspective, Jesus dying on a cross is senseless. But from God's perspective, every detail of the cross makes perfect sense. To understand what happened on the cross, you must learn to see the cross *As God Sees The Cross*. Add to your journal details that are new to you.

The Public Execution

The Promise of the Cross

If you've ever read Psalm 22 and Isaiah 53, *written hundreds of years before Christ*, you know how chillingly accurate these prophetic words are in describing the suffering Jesus endured. Our minds struggle to understand: *Why the cross? Why did Christ have to die like that?* The Old Testament holds all the answers. It is the key to the cross.

Look at **Luke 24:44-45.** These were His last moments with His disciples before Jesus was taken up into heaven before their eyes. So His last words to them would be carefully chosen and highly important, right? What did he say?

He said: *The Old Testament is all about Me!*

He *opened their minds* so they could understand the Scriptures and see that Jesus is throughout the Old Testament. *It's all about Jesus.* Everything points to Jesus. Everything teaches about Jesus. *He will open your mind* so that you can understand ... *just ask Him*!

The beautiful name for Jesus, the *"Lamb of God,"* teaches us much about what Jesus was *doing* on the cross. Let's allow the Old Testament to provide our answers. We'll have to go all the way back to the beginning, **Genesis 2:17.**

What one restriction did God place on Adam and what was the consequence for disobedience?

God made His standard very clear: disobedience is sin and sin brings death. Every Sunday School child knows the story. Adam and Eve defied God, they were seduced by Satan into disobeying and suffered painful consequences.

God was grieved and broken-hearted by their choice to sin against His goodness. Their joy and security in Paradise were replaced with fear and shame. [**Genesis 3:10**] God punished Adam, Eve and Satan for their defiance. Notice God's curse on the earth for sin recorded in **Genesis 3:17-18**. How did thorns ~ the curse of *our* sin ~ cause Jesus pain?

Adam and Eve's sin broke their fellowship with God. They deserved death; that's what God said. Is there any hope? Read **Genesis 3:21**. What did God do?

Why do you think God did that?

Something had to die to pay the cost for that sin. "The wages of sin is death." [**Romans 6:23**]. An innocent animal who never ate that fruit, who never defied God shed its blood and died as a *substitute* for Adam and Eve. In His mercy, God allowed innocent blood to be sacrificed *in their place*.

Write the result of their sin against God. [**Genesis 3:23-24**]

How did the broken fellowship affect God's heart?

Adam and Eve were forced to leave Paradise because of sin. The animal skins were a vivid reminder that **sin is serious** and yet, the Father is **merciful**. The flaming sword was a painful reminder that the intimacy God enjoyed with them was gone. There was *nothing* Adam and Eve could do to "fix" this, no way they could make peace with God for their sin.

The separation from His children was painful to God's heart. God must make peace for them. God would make peace.

In **Genesis 3:15**, God made *the Promise of a Cross:* He would send One who would crush Satan and save us.

The long wait for salvation began.

Read **Genesis 22:1-7.** Abraham and his precious Isaac ~ the only son born of God's promise, born to Abraham in his old age ~ climbed Mt. Moriah together to do the unthinkable. *God wanted Abraham to sacrifice his son as a burnt offering to God.* Isaac, a young man, carried the wood for the sacrifice on his back. One day God's own Son would carry the wood for His sacrifice, *the cross,* on His back.

Isaac questioned his father, "Where is the lamb for the sacrifice?" Write Abraham's answer in **Genesis 22:8.**

Read **Genesis 22:9-12.** Why did God stop Abraham?

God rewarded Abraham's unquestioning obedience. What did God do in **Genesis 22:13**?

"Thicket" is another name for *thorns.* How does a ram get caught in thorns? By its horns. When Abraham looked up, he saw an innocent ram standing as a substitute for Isaac caught with a *crown of thorns around his head.* What divine visual did God provide in **Genesis 22** for us to see?

The long wait for salvation continued.

A day was coming when God would provide Himself an innocent Lamb who would wear a crown of thorns. A day was coming when God would require of Himself what He did not require of Abraham ~ God *would* sacrifice His only Son. A day was coming ... and the world waited for that day.

Look again at **Exodus 12:12-13**. What does this Scripture now teach you about the work Christ would do on the cross?

The Old Testament is a divine visual of Christ.

On Mt. Sinai, God gave Moses the Law, what we call the Ten Commandments. God gave Moses something equally incredible. Moses was given a *blueprint* of the Tabernacle with instructions to build an earthly copy of what exists in heaven! **[Hebrews 8:5]** Read **Exodus 25:8**. After so many years of broken fellowship and separation, God said something astounding: "Have them make Me a tent and I will come and dwell ~ *tabernacle* ~ with them. I will live in the heart of My people, in the center of their city of tents."

There are over 40 chapters in the Bible which describe *exactly* how to construct this Tabernacle [also known as the Tent of Meeting], the types of materials and colors to use, the sizes of each piece of furniture and where to place them. If God reserved 40 chapters in His Word to teach us about the Tabernacle, *it's obviously important*!

God was slowly coming back down to man again ~~ first on top of Mt. Sinai; now down into the heart of the camp in a cloud of glory residing inside His "Tent," His Tabernacle.

How far down to man would God one day come?

At His Tabernacle God would now allow man to begin to come back into His Presence. God instituted the priesthood. [see **Exodus chapters 28 & 29**]. God allowed the priest, God's appointed representative, to approach God on behalf of the people and seek forgiveness for sin at God's altar.

The priest was required to offer something very specific at God's altar as the basis on which he could approach God and seek forgiveness. What do you think God required?

See **Leviticus 17:11** to see if you are right. What did God require to make atonement for sin?

Jesus IS the Tabernacle,
the WAY into God's Presence.

What have you learned about God's desire to have fellowship with His children?

Do you give God the time He wishes for fellowship with you? What changes are you willing to make in your life so you will have more time for *God to enjoy you* and *you to enjoy God*?

Make an entry of every way Jesus *opened your mind* to see Him in the Old Testament Scriptures. He is your Teacher.

Walking the Blood Path

It must have been difficult for the Jewish leaders to contain their smugness as they watched the last minute preparations for another Roman crucifixion. But this was not just another crucifixion ~ because the One about to be crucified was that blasphemer who claimed to be the Son of God. The soldiers gathered their supplies while the sign bearing the charge was made ready:

"**Jesus of Nazareth, The King of The Jews.**"

The sign would either be hung around the neck of the accused or displayed at the front of a grisly parade. Roman prisoners were dragged through the streets in a public display of cruelty with a clear message: *"This could happen to you."* The procession would wind through the streets and outside the city gates to Golgotha, known as *the Place of the Skull.* There, in full view of passersby and in total shame like a common criminal, Jesus of Nazareth would hang on a cross.

Remember at the Passover supper, Jesus sang aloud, "I will fulfill my vow to the LORD in the presence of all the people." As His battered body left a trail of crimson blood that would stain the streets of Jerusalem, *the city of God,* Jesus would also fulfill **the vow of the LORD**.

Many centuries earlier, God called a man named Abram to leave his homeland and be the father of a new nation. God made a vow to Abram; *today Jesus would keep that vow.*

Read **Genesis 12:1-3** to discover God's promise to Abram. Write the last very important phrase of God's promise.

Later God changed Abram's name to Abraham. What nation do you think God was about to begin?

Imagine, God promised "all peoples will be blessed through you" and your descendants will be as numerous as the stars! Any idea what God was planning that would be so incredible as to *bless every person in the world*?

God promised Abram this nation would have God's blessings and the right under God's authority to the land of Canaan. [**Genesis 13:14-17**] This nation would have the distinct honor of being God's people, and would be expected to be set apart, *holy,* as belonging to God.

God sealed His *covenant* with Abram the way two parties would make a contract in that day. It was a practice known as *walking the blood path.* Our method of "signing on the dotted line" is a bit easier and a lot less messy.

Read **Genesis 15:7-11.** Two parties making a covenant would gather the animals, cut them in half lengthwise and place the animals on opposite sides of a hillside. As you can imagine, the blood of the animals would flow down and form a puddle of blood in the middle. The two parties then walked the blood path hand in hand, as a declaration that "If I do not keep my covenant with you, I will die; I will pay with my blood." Abram obeyed God and assembled the animals. Then something unexpected happened in **Genesis 15:12-21.** As the sun was setting, what did Abram do?

When darkness had fallen, what happened?

"On that day the LORD made a covenant with Abram." It is commonly referred to in the Bible as *the Old Covenant*. But what part did Abram play in the covenant? None! Abram was asleep! "When God made His promise to Abraham, since there was no one greater for him to swear by, He swore by himself." **[Hebrews 6:13]** God vowed that if Abraham and his descendants broke the covenant, God would come and die in their place. *God would pay with His blood.*

God walked the blood path alone.

Today Jesus would fulfill the vow of the Lord. Jesus would walk the blood path and pay with His blood. God's own Son was paraded through the streets of Jerusalem in **our** shame, carrying the wood for His sacrifice on His back. Do you remember who else carried wood for his sacrifice on his back picturing what Christ would do one day? **[Genesis 22:6]**

The streets were busy. Tomorrow was Sabbath so the marketplace was overflowing with shoppers and peddlers. Before the grisly parade made its way out of the city, it would pass through the meat market. *On the way to the cross, Jesus walked through a slaughterhouse.*

What significance should that have for us?

Jesus would bleed seven times during His prolonged agony. He sweat droplets of blood in the Garden of Gethsemane; He bled from His back as they flogged him with a whip;

from His head when they placed the crown of thorns; from His right wrist; from His left wrist; from His feet and from His side. Throughout the Bible, seven is God's number of completeness, of His perfection; i.e. seven days of creation. Seven times the perfect blood of Christ bled for us.

The perfect blood of Jesus stained Jerusalem's soil from Pilate's court all the way to the cross. He walked a painful path, a shameful path. *He walked the blood path.* He fulfilled the vow of the LORD because we broke the Covenant and turned our back on God.

The Son of God walked the blood path alone.

Why do you think God made this Old Covenant with Abram?

What does the *blood path* teach about the character of God?

How has He proven Himself to be faithful?

How should this affect the daily choices you make? Is your desire to remain holy and faithful to Him an overriding factor in how you have been living your life? If not, what practical changes could you make?

Jot down everything new you learned from the Old Testament in this lesson. Include your observations about the character of God.

The Daily Sacrifice

When we understand the significance of the sacrifices that God required the Jewish people to offer to Him on the altar, then we begin to see the cross *"As God Sees the Cross."*

Being a priest in God's "tent" was serious business! God was *very specific* about how things were done in His Tabernacle. If man was to be allowed back into God's Presence again, he would have to come by God's terms. Imagine the anticipation among the people when God's first High Priest, Aaron [the brother of Moses], approached God's "tent" to be consecrated and begin work.

Read **Leviticus 9:5-8** to see that all the people of Israel *stood before the Lord* ~ a sign of reverence.

What did God promise would be the result of obeying His commands *exactly*?

That's certainly incentive for getting it right! God would use the sacrifices on the altar to teach His people how to obtain forgiveness. What did Aaron have to do personally, as High Priest, before sacrificing an offering to God for the people?

What did God require the priest to *do* with the blood offered as his sin offering? **See Leviticus 9:9.**

If His commands were followed exactly, God promised that the "altar will be most holy, and whatever touches it will be holy." [**Exodus 29:37**] They were given the privilege to approach God at His altar. They would soon discover the altar was not only a holy place but a *busy* place. **Read Exodus 29:38-39.** Record what God required and how often.

Every morning at 9:00 a.m. and every evening at 3:00 p.m. God required a sacrifice. At 3:00 p.m. the sound of the ***shofar*** [a curled ram's horn] would be heard, signifying that at that moment the lamb was dying as an offering to God. This daily offering was "a pleasing aroma" to the Lord, according to **Exodus 29:41.**

For what *reason* do you think it was pleasing to God?

Knowing its significance, when the people heard the ***shofar*** sound daily at 3:00 p.m, what heart response do you think was appropriate?

For centuries the priests offered daily sacrifices, day after day, to obtain God's forgiveness~ first for themselves and then for the people. For centuries, God's prophets brought His message to the people: *be ready*, because one day God's own blood would be offered as the evening sacrifice. For centuries, the people waited for Messiah to save them.

After centuries of waiting, the day of God's promise arrived. When the shofar sounded on this day, *creation would shake*.

Read **Mark 15:21-32**. The grisly parade arrived at Golgotha. Make a list of the individuals or groups of people named and their interactions with Jesus.

What time did they place Christ on the cross? Hint: the start of the *Jewish* day was 6:00 a.m.

Why did God plan for Christ to be placed on the cross at *that* time of day? *As God Sees the Cross*, what was He seeing?

From 9:00 a.m. until 12:00 noon, man did his worst to Christ as He hung on that cross in *our* shame. He was surrounded by mockers ~ robbers scorned Him on either side, the chief priests and teachers of the law hurled insults, and the Roman centurion in charge sat indifferently at the foot of the cross waiting for Him to die. But the horror was about to begin.

Read **Mark 15:33**. Something significant happened; what was it and what time did it occur?

What do you think God was conveying to the world?

*At noon darkness fell on that cross
and it became an altar.*

God pulled down a veil of darkness because what happened on that cross was too awful to be looked upon. It was a transaction between Father and Son. Judgment for sin under cover of darkness ~ so fitting because under cover of darkness sin does its worst damage. On that altar the world got a glimpse of hell, *the agony of man's soul without God.*
The Light of the World was being extinguished and the world turned dark. God poured out on Jesus His wrath against sin; then turned His back as the Precious Lamb of God "took away the sin of the world" on that altar. [**John 1:29**]

When would this agony end? Read **Mark 15:33-34.** Knowing 6:00-7:00 a.m. is the first hour, what time is it now?

What is about to happen at God's altar in the temple as it does every day?

Turn to **John 19:30** and write the familiar phrase Christ cried out from the cross *when the shofar sounded.*

What do you think Christ was referring to?

Look at one last verse, **Luke 22:20**, and remember Jesus' words at the *cup of salvation.* Any new thoughts?

That *shofar* sounding heralded the end of the Old Covenant. The endless daily sacrifice of lambs at the altar is finished.
The Lamb of God offered the perfect sacrifice,
one sacrifice for all sin for all time.

It is finished!

God promised in **Leviticus 9:6** that when God's command was obeyed and the sacrifice was offered *exactly* as God said, *the glory of the LORD would appear.* Watch and see the glory of the LORD appear as God responds to the perfect sacrifice offered by the Lamb of God!

As God Sees the Cross, what does He see?

How is Jesus truly the "Lamb of God" for each of us?

Something else happened on the cross that day and the pieces of another pattern fit together! Genesis 2 is the story of the first bridegroom and bride. Read **Genesis 2:21-22** to see what God did.

Out of Adam's side, God "birthed" Adam's bride. God would "birth" another Bride the same way. Read **John 19:32-34**. What did the soldiers do to Jesus? What flowed as a result?

Do you remember the costly price God required of Jesus, as the *Bridegroom*, in order to purchase His Bride, His Church? [see page 33]

Our Bridegroom sacrificed His life for His Bride. When they pierced His side, that flowing blood and water confirmed the death of the Bridegroom and the birth of His Bride. Out of His side came the lifeblood of the Church.

> *Deliver them from sin & death with your blood.*
> *Offer yourself as Passover Lamb for them.*

~~~~~~~

Add to your journal each new thing you learned about the cross. Include ways you now see the cross differently.

The Cries from the Cross

The last words spoken to someone you love deeply are carefully chosen words meant to be remembered forever. In the midst of physical and spiritual agony, Jesus spoke His *last words* from the cross. Words spoken with purpose. Words meant to be remembered. Seven times He spoke. Seven is God's number of completeness, of His perfection. In the seven cries of Christ from the cross, we see the complete perfection of a loving God saving His children.

In His three-year ministry on earth, Jesus poured out His love on everyone. He loved the unlovable. He touched the untouchable. He lifted up the beaten down. He made whole the broken bodies. *He wept for love of them.* They responded to His love with a frightening display of how truly evil man's heart is. *May we never become casual about the suffering Jesus endured on that cross for us.*

His first words will take your breath away. As you read **Luke 23:34,** allow yourself to picture what Jesus looked like as He hung on that cross. Write them and remember them.

His first word is *"Abba,"* the tender Hebrew name for Daddy. Was the trauma so overwhelming that He reverted to the childhood name of His Father? "Daddy, forgive them..."

Forgive them??? But they are selfish, peevish, foolish. Evil, deceitful, sinful. *You can forgive them*?

What do those words reveal to us about the heart of God?

Perhaps **1 John 4:10** can help us understand the heart of God. What prompts God's desire to forgive and save His children?

Jesus set the divine standard of forgiveness and God expects the same response from us. Can any offense against us be greater than the agony of the cross? Why does God expect you to forgive? See **Colossians 3:13**.

Has someone committed an offense against you that remains unforgiven? Ask God to give you a heart to forgive them; then restore the relationship. In doing so, you will honor God.

Luke 23:39-43 tells the story of the two criminals crucified with Jesus. Each criminal made a true statement about Jesus. What did each say, and what request did one make of Jesus?

What do Jesus' second words from the cross teach us about Him and about those who believe in Him? **[Luke 23:43]**

Read **John 11:25** to recall the powerful promise Jesus gave for those who believe in Him. How does Jesus describe Himself?

Jesus asks: "Do you believe this?" What is your response?

Do you?

It was just before noon. Jesus **knew** every agony He would endure on the cross. He knew God's wrath was about to be poured out on Him for our sin. What do you think Jesus had on His mind? *You may be surprised.* See **John 19:26-27**. What did Jesus do?

Read **Deuteronomy 5:16**. Jesus set an example of obedience. What was He obeying and why?

By honoring our mother and father, we honor our Father in heaven.

The fourth and most passionate cry from the cross came just before 3:00. The spiritual suffering reached an intensity that overwhelmed Him. Read **Matthew 27:46**. What do you think was happening that caused Jesus to cry out?

The weight of every sin committed by every person who will ever live ~ how heavy is that weight? Add to that the guilt, the shame, the painful consequences of all that sin. Then pour on top the righteous wrath of a Holy, Perfect and Almighty God against every sin, because every sin that we commit is *an offense against God.*

How heavy is that weight now?   How ugly?   How vile?
It is so vile that Almighty God cannot and will not look upon it. When Jesus hung on that cross in darkness for three hours, He hung there *totally alone*.

He experienced the spiritual agony awaiting everyone who refuses to believe in Jesus ~ eternal separation from God. Jesus took on Himself the horror of eternity in hell for every person that will ever live ~ and experienced it in three hours.

Read **John 3:16-18**. What is the good news for those who believe in Jesus? What is the sober warning to those who do not believe?

Do you believe in the Name of God's one and only Son?

It is very close to 3:00 and the last three cries from the cross come quickly. The fifth cry is recorded in **John 19:28-29**.
What does Jesus say and why does He say it?

Intense thirst is one of the painful effects of crucifixion. The wine vinegar Jesus was given moistened His mouth so He could loudly cry out two last times.

The powerful sixth cry came as the ***shofar*** sounded. The daily sacrifice was being offered and the lamb was dying. Write the words **The Lamb** triumphantly cried out from the cross.

Read again **John 19:30**. List those things that we have already learned are now finished!

It didn't matter that Israel's high priest had torn his clothes. There was no longer a need for daily sacrifices. There was no longer a need for a high priest. We had something better!

Discover what we now have by reading **Hebrews 4:14-16**. How is Jesus described?

We have a *Great High Priest* who has gone through the heavens! We have everything we need in Him! Based on the sinless perfection of Jesus, what are we invited to do?

It is finished! The Old Covenant is finished. The death sentence over man since Adam and Eve in the Garden of Eden is finished. The separation between God and man is finished. The flaming sword that prevented Adam and Eve from approaching God is extinguished. It is **all** finished! Look once more at **Luke 23:43**. What place has been opened again?

The joy of being with Jesus ~ Paradise

The seventh and last cry is recorded in **Luke 23:46**. Jesus again cries to "Abba." What do you find significant about how Jesus dies? What is special about His voice?

He had done all that His Father required of Him.
He was obedient and sinless.
He offered Himself as the perfect sacrifice.
He paid the Bride Price with His blood.

Then He willingly, victoriously, voluntarily placed His life in His Father's hands. No one took it from Him. *He gave it.*

His seven cries from the cross are examples for us to follow. Examples of forgiveness, perfect love, obedience, and the victory that is ours in Jesus!

Which of the seven cries caused the strongest response from you? Why?

Hearing Jesus cry, *"My God, My God, why have You forsaken Me?"* is almost unbearable, isn't it? But in those painful words are the *proof* that Jesus *did* take our sin on Him. It's *gone!*

Psalm 130:3 *says:*
*"If you, O LORD, kept a record of sins,
O LORD, who could stand?
But with You there is forgiveness; therefore, You are feared."*

You are forgiven in Jesus.

Stand up!   Thank Him!

By now your list is growing. Record everything you've learned, every point you want to remember.

The Eternal Resurrection

The Earth Shook

His exhausted followers were stunned. They had heard the victorious "death cry" of Jesus split the air, followed by a palpable silence. God's heart erupted as the Son whom He loves gave His life and *"at that moment" the earth shook.* Read **Matthew 27:51-53**. List the five points mentioned.

"The curtain of the temple was torn in two from top to bottom." Seems like an insignificant detail when compared to the earth shaking and bodies coming out of tombs, right? Actually, *that curtain tearing caused the earth to shake*!

Where do we go to find out about this "curtain" in the temple? The Old Testament is the key to the cross. All our answers are right there waiting.

The Tabernacle, God's "tent" in the wilderness, was designed and constructed to be a temporary structure. Each time God's cloud of glory moved, Israel had to be ready to dismantle the Tabernacle and follow. God very specifically assigned duties to the tribes of Israel as to who carried what, and *nobody touched anything unless God said so.* Some pieces nobody could touch at all; God designed them with rings on the end, through which poles were inserted so that a group of four priests could carry it easily on their shoulders and not violate God's directions by touching it.

The study of The Tabernacle is a study of Jesus. Every detail, every color, every piece of furniture ~ everything highlights a facet of the salvation work of Jesus on the cross.

The Tabernacle was divided into two areas. The larger area, called The Holy Place, was 30' long, 15' wide and 15' high. The priests ministered to God according to His precise directions in The Holy Place. Beyond that was a perfect cube-shaped 15' area called The Holy of Holies, or literally *The Holy Holy*, because God's Presence dwelt there.

Read **Exodus 26:31-33**. What symbol is worked into the curtain? What does God say is the purpose of the curtain?

After their 40-year punishment in the wilderness ended, the Jewish nation finally entered their "Promised Land" and settled down. A magnificent temple for God was built ~ a permanent "Tabernacle." Though the Temple was built on a *much* larger scale, every color, every piece of furniture, every detail down to the symbol on the curtain was identical to the Tabernacle. God's "tent" was now a permanent structure.

Any thoughts why God placed that curtain, or veil, there?

Look again at **Genesis 3:23-24**. What had God placed on the east side of the Garden of Eden? In light of Adam and Eve's defiance of God, what was the message to His children?

God's message from the Garden of Eden until Jesus hung on the cross was the same ~ you sinned against Me and are forbidden to come into My Presence. There is a barrier that separates us; a cherubim at the entrance to God's Garden in Eden and a cherubim on a curtain at the entrance to *The Holy Holy* where God was.

A barrier separated us ... until this day! Something incredible happened to a massive curtain well over 20' high and half a foot thick, a curtain that took many priests to wrestle with it. "At that moment" when Christ died and the sin penalty was finally paid in full, God reached down and *ripped that curtain from top to bottom!* What was God saying?

Centuries of painful separation from God have finally ended. The barrier is gone and something wonderful is in its place. Read **1 Timothy 2:5** and **Hebrews 9:14-15**. What role does Jesus now play for us?

God was willing to welcome His children back into His Paradise. As long as they came through His Son.

The earth shook! It wasn't the first time the earth shook while Jesus walked on the earth. Look back again to **Matthew 21:10**. It tells the events of a very special day earlier that week. Do you remember what it was called?

Matthew said "the whole city was *stirred*" ~ using the Greek word from which we get earthquake! Creation shook at the Lamb's triumphal entry into the city and shook again at the Lamb's triumphal *death! Creation responds to its Creator.*

The tombs broke open! Dead people walking around again! What do you think, were they really alive again?

Take a minute to read a powerful story in **John 11:1-44**. Pay special attention to the end of verse 4, verse 25 and verse 40. Had Jesus ever brought anyone out of a grave to life?

This miracle pointed forward to the Resurrection when Jesus would walk out of a grave to *eternal life*. It was a foretaste of God's promise that because Jesus lives, anyone who believes in the Name of the Son of God will live forever with Him.

Remember reading **Leviticus 9:6**. How would God respond if His Son's sacrifice was carried out *exactly* as He commanded?

List the ways God's glory was seen the day Jesus died.

If you believe, you will see the glory of God.

Did the creatures respond to the Creator as powerfully as His creation did? Well, some did; some didn't. It may surprise us to learn who! Read **Mark 15:38-39**. Who is Mark talking about, where is he standing, and what conclusion does he come to?

Remember who this is ~ he's the Roman soldier in charge of the crucifixion. It started out as just another day on the job, sitting at the foot of the cross until this Jewish guy dies.

The Bible doesn't tell us, but how do you think his work day ended?

Luke 23:48-49 tells of two other groups and their responses. Who comprised the first group? Record their response.

Who comprised the second group? Record their response.

What factor made the difference in how people responded?

His devastated disciples would find comfort by remembering what Jesus prayed near the end of that Passover supper. Read again **John 17:1-5.** His followers had learned to know the only true God and *know Jesus Christ*, whom God had sent, and so they stayed. And just as Jesus had prayed in verse 5, *they would see the Father glorify the Son.*

A Roman soldier standing at the foot of that cross *looked at the evidence* before him and believed He was seeing the Son of God. *Are you looking closely at the evidence?*

Add any new understanding of Scripture and new thoughts to your journal.

A Sign in a Secure Tomb

Jesus of Nazareth was dead. That news brought a mixed response. Some were indifferent; it was just another Jewish fanatic. Some were ecstatic; their enemy had been defeated. Some were distraught; they lost the One they loved, their Lord.

Read **Matthew 27:57-61**. Who comes forward to ask for the body of Jesus and is he successful?

List the additional information we learn about this man from **Mark 15:42-45** and **John 19:38**.

The Council is another name for the Sanhedrin. What risk was Joseph of Arimathea taking by his action?

How does Pilate confirm Jesus is dead? See **Mark 15:44-45**.

Everybody agreed Jesus was DEAD. Pilate knew it. The Jewish leaders knew it. His followers knew it. He was DEAD. His body was removed from the cross and given to His followers to be prepared for burial. Time was not on their side, because it would soon be Sabbath. In obedience to God's Sabbath law, the extensive anointing with spices would have to wait until the day after the Sabbath. **[Luke 23:55-56]**

Jesus is dead, lying in Joseph of Arimathea's tomb. What does **Matthew 27:59-60** tell us about the security of the tomb?

Tombs were usually cut in the rock hillside at the lower edge. A large stone would be rolled downward and gravity would bring it to rest over the entrance of the tomb, sealing it securely. Since Joseph of Arimathea was a wealthy prominent man, we can assume the tomb was secured by the followers of Jesus in this manner.

The chief priests and Pharisees should be pleased, right? But apparently they weren't kicking back and enjoying a victory dinner. God would use their plotting to verify a crucial piece of the Resurrection story! Read **Matthew 27:62-66**; the day after Preparation Day was Saturday, the Sabbath. What do they ask of Pilate and what is done to the tomb?

What were they worried about? Record what they have just unwittingly done by their actions!

The followers of Jesus spent their Sabbath huddled together in sorrow. They had forgotten Jesus' repeated prophetic promise that He would rise again. What had Jesus said only hours earlier on the way to the Garden of Gethsemane that they didn't remember? See **Matthew 26:32**.

Nobody was expecting what awaited them on Sunday morning! Even though Jesus told them clearly at least four times that He would rise from the dead, [see **Matthew 16:21, 17:22-23, 20:18-19** and **26:32**] the disciples just never understood!!! There was never a question of them stealing the body of Jesus or making up a story about Jesus rising from the dead ~~ because they weren't expecting it to happen! The gospel writers very honestly stated: we didn't get it! [see **John 10:6, John 11:13** and **John 20:9** as examples]

If the disciples weren't intending to steal the body or make up a story that the body was stolen, what is incredibly ironic about what the chief priests and leaders did?

Sunday morning dawns, the first day of the week, and women are on their way to the tomb with spices. Three women, one of whom was Mary Magdalene, go ahead of the others, wondering how they will move the stone. What do they discover when they arrive? [see **John 20:1-2**]   What action does Mary Magdalene take?

What reaction does she receive and why? See **Luke 24:9-11**.

Read the gospel accounts found in **Matthew 27:59-61, Mark 15:46-47, Luke 23:55** and **John 19:39-42**. Make a list of the people who *know exactly where that tomb is*.

How likely do you think it is that they were at the wrong tomb?

In the foot race back to the tomb, John arrives first, then Peter; after they leave, Mary Magdalene returns. Each will discover something startling! Read **John 20:3-9** [John is "the other disciple."] Who went in the tomb and what did he see?

What does John tell us about his reaction? **John 20:8**.

Luke 24:12 tells us that Peter went away wondering to himself. That's because Peter saw a sign when he looked in that tomb that left him shaking in his sandals! What we read over as a minor detail was actually a powerful sign.

Bodies prepared for burial would be wrapped tightly with strips of linen layered with many pounds of spices until they looked like a mummy. The head would be wrapped with a separate piece of linen, commonly referred to as a "napkin."
A Jewish rabbi's head, however, would be wrapped with his beautiful prayer shawl. Jewish rabbis had a special way of meticulously folding their prayer shawl that set them apart.

In Eastern customs, when the "master" was called away during a meal, if he was finished the meal he would simply drop the napkin beside his plate and leave. However, if the "master" was called away and planned to return, he would carefully fold his napkin and place it away from his plate.

This recognizable sign from the "master" to the servant signified: *"I am not finished; I am coming back."* Read with interest what John notes in **John 20:6-7**. What did Peter see?

To a Jew looking into that tomb, it was clear that the last one in that tomb was a Jew. Not only a Jew, but a Jewish rabbi who folded that prayer shawl and placed it away by itself!
What message do you think Jesus was leaving for them?

No wonder Peter went away wondering to himself ...

After Peter and John leave, Mary Magdalene arrives again at the tomb. She sees an even more incredible sign. To "see" what Mary saw, we need to return to the Old Testament.

We've already looked at **Exodus 25:8** in *The Promise of the Cross,* but now we'll dig a little deeper! On Mt. Sinai, after God told Moses to build Him a "tent," He began to give Moses blueprints for the Tabernacle. He told Moses about *the most important* furnishing in the Tabernacle first.

Read **Exodus 25:10-16**. God gives Moses very specific instructions and measurements. What does God tell Moses to build? If you can, figure out how big it was.

This beautiful chest of wood overlaid with pure gold is known as the Ark of the Covenant. God said to put the Ten Commandments, known as "The Ark of the Testimony," inside the chest. God also required a special lid for this chest. Read **Exodus 25:17-21**. Describe God's very specific instructions for placement of the *cherubim*, or angels, atop the lid.

The Jewish people called this chest The Ark of the Covenant. They called the pure gold atonement lid *The Mercy Seat*. Remember: this Tabernacle is an earthly copy of what is in heaven! **[Hebrews 8:5]**

Read God's astounding words to Moses in **Exodus 25:22**. Moses must have been speechless! God announced that it was here, at the Mercy Seat between the two angels facing each other, that *the very Presence of God would dwell and the people would obtain mercy for their sins.*

The Ark of the Covenant with its solid gold Mercy Seat on top was **the only piece of furniture** placed beyond the curtain in the Holy of Holies, or *The Holy Holy*, in God's Tabernacle.

Knowing the Old Testament significance, what you are about to read will jump off the page at you! Read **John 20:10-12** and "see" what Mary Magdalene saw in the place where Jesus' body had been. Write what she saw.

In actuality, what did that slab on which they placed the body of the Son of God become?

The Ark with its atonement lid known as The Mercy Seat is one of hundreds of Old Testament "pictures" of Jesus. Inside the Ark lay the Ten Commandments, which we continually sinned against by breaking and which convicted us to death. On top was The Mercy Seat, where mercy covered over our "death sentence." The tomb where Jesus' body lay with an angel at the head and an angel at the foot, with their wings touching in the middle, was *the true Mercy Seat* on earth.

At that tomb God showed us mercy. Jesus died in our place. When God raised Jesus back to life, He raised us with Him.

Because He lives, we live!

Why do you think God filled the Old Testament with "pictures" that pointed to what Jesus would do for us on the cross?

We have sinned against God, our loving Father. Yet, in His compassion He is anxious to forgive us and offer His mercy. *As God Sees the Cross*, He sees His Son and forgives us.

Suppose you allowed your own son to suffer physical pain in order to help someone else's child. Wouldn't you expect them to *at least* be grateful? How would you feel if they chose to ignore your son's gift and treated him with contempt?

How do you think God feels?

As you continue compiling your list of new information, notice how much of it is coming from the Old Testament!

Atonement

Mary Magdalene stands outside the empty tomb weeping. The angels sitting where the body of Jesus once was ask her why she is crying. *Why is she crying?* Her world has been ripped apart. Her Lord hung on a cross right before her eyes and as He died the earth shook. Now she comes to the tomb where He lay, only to find Him gone? *Who has answers?*

A "gardener" nearby asked her a second time why she is crying. We can almost imagine her screaming out, "*I just want my Jesus!*" Mary blessed the heart of Jesus, standing there desperately seeking only one thing: Him! God rewards those who seek Him; He delights in those who pursue Him.

Jesus rewarded Mary's display of genuine, broken-hearted love for Him. Jesus met her right there and showed Himself to Mary *first*. Mary was the first to hear that voice and see that face again. Read **John 20:10-18**.

What did Mary tell the gardener she would do once she knew where Jesus was?

Instead, what happened?

We don't have to "go get Him." He responds immediately to our need for Him. Jesus comes to us *right where we are*. Have you ever wondered: *Where are you, Jesus, when I need You?* Sometimes, like Mary, our spiritual eyes don't "see" Him when He's right there! Are you calling out His Name?

What did the voice of Jesus sound like when Mary heard Him speak her name? We can imagine it sounded the same way it will sound to each of us when, one day, we shall see Him face to face and hear Him speak our name...

Unspeakable joy! Mary was *the first to see Jesus* and wanted to hold onto Him forever! But what does Jesus tell her?

What are your thoughts as to why?

You may know from **Matthew 28:8-9** that the other women with the spices "clasped His feet and worshiped Him." Why did Jesus not allow Mary Magdalene to touch Him? The answer is found ~ you knew it, didn't you! ~ in the Old Testament.

God teaches us so much about Jesus in the Old Testament. The Tabernacle with its altar for burnt offerings, the kinds of sacrifices to be offered there, the instructions for what must be done with the blood of the lamb, the priests and their service in God's "tent" house, the feast days to be celebrated and their meaning ~~ all are pattern pieces God wants us to see. Each one adds another layer to the meaning of the cross.

The overriding theme of the Old Testament is man's need for forgiveness from God. The tragedy in the Garden of Eden sentenced every person to death. God promised a Savior, but He wanted us to understand what the Savior would do. *God was going to give His Son; He expected us to appreciate why.*

Are you beginning to appreciate the cross in a new way based on what God has been showing you in the Old Testament?

Take a quick peek at **Exodus 28**. God told Moses on Mt. Sinai what the priestly wardrobe would be ~ costly! Many precious jewels in pure gold filigree settings. Garments woven by skilled craftsmen with gold threads. A royal diadem. Each article of clothing taught a lesson about God's character. The High Priest was to dress befitting the high calling of serving God!

One day of the year, however, the High Priest would dress differently. This special day was the *Day of Atonement*.
Read **Leviticus 16:3-4**. What did God say Aaron, the High Priest, should do and what should he wear?

He would wear only simple sacred garments on this day because today the priest *goes into the very Presence of God* in total humility. Look at **Leviticus 16:2**. What does God warn is the consequence of getting this wrong?

Aaron couldn't come whenever he chose [**Leviticus 16:2**] , but on the Day of Atonement where was he told to go? [**verse 12**]

God required Aaron to have something with him that *allowed him access beyond the veil* into the Most Holy Place where God was. Any ideas? [see **Leviticus 16:14-17**]

Aaron was required to make two offerings, the first for his personal sins; the second for the sins of the nation of Israel. He was to pour out some of the blood in front of the atonement cover [the *Mercy Seat*] and then to sprinkle the remaining blood seven times on top of that atonement cover. Do you remember what was inside the ark with the atonement cover lid? [see page 99]

God not only required the High Priest to dress specifically for this Day of Atonement; He also commanded something else. What does **Leviticus 16:23** require him to do?

According to **Leviticus 16:34**, how often were they to celebrate this day and what was its purpose?

Every year this solemn day had to be repeated. Why? Because *the blood offered was not perfect blood*. God in His mercy would accept this blood as a "promissory note" to cover their sin for one year ... until the One with perfect blood, the Great High Priest, would come and offer a permanent sacrifice.

Peek again into that empty tomb. We see the prayer shawl folded separately; what else is lying there? **[John 20:6]**

What "garment" did Jesus wear into that tomb? **[John 19:40]**

What "garment" did our Great High Priest obediently leave on the *Mercy Seat* in that tomb?

Read again what Jesus said when He first appeared to Mary. **[John 20:17]** What was He going to do?

Now look back to His words at the Passover Supper, when He lifted the *cup of salvation* and asked each of us to be His spiritual bride. What did Jesus say? [see **Matthew 26:27-28**]

Where did God require the blood to be *poured out* in order to make atonement ~ forgiveness ~ for sin?

Remember the earthly Tabernacle was a copy of God's throne room in heaven. Look at **Hebrews 9:23-28.**

Where do you think Jesus went after He appeared to Mary and what did He do with His blood?

Jesus left His linen garment at the Mercy Seat on earth, the tomb where the angels sat facing each other with wings touching. He stood before His Father at *the* Tabernacle in heaven. The Son presented His perfect blood to the Father. Then our Great High Priest poured out His blood by sprinkling that life-saving blood seven perfect times, covering over the Law that condemned us and making atonement for us.

The day of the cross is the true Day of Atonement.
Jesus made peace for us. We are at one with God again.

at-one-ment

As God sees the blood on the mercy seat, He sees the cross.
As God Sees the Cross, He sees His Son.
It is *because* of Who His Son is that God forgives us.

There is only one way to God's heart. There is only one way to receive forgiveness from God. It is through the blood of His Son. Look again at **Leviticus 16:2**. What did God warn would be the result if Aaron ~ or anyone ~ approaches God without protection of the blood of Jesus?

The perfect blood of Jesus is eternally in God's holy presence.
It is the basis on which we approach God. It is the basis on which we present our praises and prayers unto God's throne.

God looks on the blood of Jesus and *answers your cry*.

Are you covered by the blood of Jesus? It doesn't happen automatically. It is a choice. It is a free gift that must be asked for and accepted. Just as a beautifully wrapped package becomes yours when you open it and receive it, so it is with salvation. It is a free gift for you. **[Ephesians 2:8]**
A gift wrapped in the most beautiful package to God's eyes
~ the blood of Jesus ~

There is only one question in life of eternal importance and that is this: "What must I do to be saved?" **[Acts 16:30]** The answer is simple: "Believe in the Lord Jesus and you will be saved." **[Acts 16:31]**

Are you ready to receive your free gift of salvation? All God requires is a sincere sorrow in your heart for your sins and a sincere desire in your heart for Him.

Why not pray this prayer to Him right where you are:

"Dear God, I know that I have sinned against You. I have not led a perfect life and I cannot. I understand now that I can't make my sins right in your eyes because it takes perfect blood to do that. I'm beginning to understand Your Word. You love me and want me to be with You. I believe that Jesus is Your Son, the Messiah You promised. I thank you that Jesus died on that cross for my sin. *I ask you, Jesus, to be My Savior.* I invite You to live in my heart forever and I promise to give my heart to You. Change me and make me like You. I know that based on Your promise, one day I will live with you forever.
Thank you, Father, for loving me enough to save me.
In the Name of Jesus I pray.
Amen."

If you chose to pray that prayer, the angels in heaven are rejoicing over you right now! **[Luke 15:7]** You have just been "born again" to live eternally with Jesus.

~~~~~~

Make notes so you'll remember the many ways God revealed Jesus in the Old Testament.

One last lesson remains and then we have finished.
You have honored God
by spending time studying the Bible.

Powerful Evidence

Jesus is alive again! Mary Magdalene can't contain herself! She runs to find Peter and John and share her good news. [Did you know that's what "gospel" means ~~ good news.] And it is indeed good news to tell someone about Jesus.

Peter and John will be thrilled when Mary brings her news, right? Read **Luke 24:11** again; what was their response?

Peter and John did not believe. You couldn't get any closer to Jesus than the disciples had walked; yet they didn't believe that Jesus had risen! It's a sad reality, but there are people sitting in churches today that are *close* ~ sitting close to the altar, close to the cross on the stained glass window, and yet do not believe Jesus is risen and *He is our only way to heaven.*

The Jewish leaders refused to believe. They refused to believe Jesus was their Messiah, the Son of God, or that He rose from the dead. In spite of all the miraculous signs He performed among them, they *refused to believe*. Read **Numbers 14:11**. When we refuse to believe, how does God view that?

Peter got up unbelieving and ran to the tomb to see*; he went away wondering to himself.* [**Luke 24:12**] That's what happens to every person who sincerely wants to see ~ the evidence provokes a response!   Because the evidence presented in the Bible is so powerful, it speaks for itself.

Do you believe that Christ rose from the dead? That is the basis, the foundation of the Christian faith. If God did not raise Christ from the dead back to life, what does that mean for us?

1 Corinthians 15:13-19 says that if Christ has not been raised, our faith is futile because we are still in our sins ~ so we are still convicted. The "wages of sin is death" so what hope do we have? If only for this life we have hope, then we are to be pitied more than all men. *But if Christ indeed rose from the dead, we have hope not only for this life ~ but for eternal life!*

I ask again: *Do you believe that Christ rose from the dead?*

God provided many powerful proofs in His Word which present an overwhelming testimony that it happened. Do you know what they are? *You need to!* They are the evidence that Your Savior is alive, seated at the right hand of His Father, making intercession right now for you in heaven.

We will look at seven of the many proofs. Then you will know what you believe, and you will be equipped to run like Mary and tell the "good news" with authority!

Jesus was publicly executed.

Everyone agreed He was dead. Pilate summoned the Roman centurion in charge of the crucifixion and confirmed that it was so. **[Mark 15:44-45]** The Jewish leaders went to Pilate asking that the tomb be guarded, saying, "We remember that while that deceiver *was alive*, He said, 'After three days I will rise again.'" It was officially declared by Pilate: **Jesus was dead**.

The tomb was secure.

Pilate complied with the request of the Jewish leaders. "Take a guard. Go, make the tomb as secure as you know how." **[Matthew 27:65.]**

Based on what you have learned about these Jewish leaders, how secure do you think they made that tomb?

Do you know the consequences for a guard to let a prisoner escape? [see **Acts 16:25-27**; God miraculously rescued Paul and Silas from prison; what was that guard about to do when he thought the prisoners had escaped?]

The tomb was empty.

The guards went into the city and reported to the chief priests *everything that had happened.*

See **Matthew 28:12-14**. What story did the chief priests instruct the guards to tell and what does it confirm?

Read **Matthew 28:15**. How did the chief priests satisfy the soldiers for doing what they were instructed?

How did the chief priests satisfy Judas for handing over Jesus?

How do you think they planned to satisfy the governor?

Many people saw Jesus alive again.

He appeared over a period of forty days to many people:
>to individuals like Mary Magdalene and Peter;
>to the small group of Eleven remaining disciples;
>to groups as large as 500 at one time.

He appeared at different times of day, in different places, and to many different people. These are just a sampling. The Bible records ten of the appearances Jesus made over those forty days. Many people saw Jesus alive again.

Many of the individuals who saw Jesus alive were still alive at the time the Holy Spirit wrote these Scriptures through Matthew, Mark, Luke, John and Paul. [**1 Corinthians 15:6**]

If this information was a "story," as the Jewish leaders tried to intimate, how do you think the people would have responded to these writings?

There was a profound change in the apostles after seeing Jesus alive.

These simple men became unstoppable!

They were imprisoned but kept on preaching.
>[**Acts 16:16-34** is one of many]

They were flogged & rejoiced to suffer for the Name of Jesus.
>[**Acts 5:40-41** is one of many]

They never stopped teaching and proclaiming the Good News that Jesus is the Christ! [**Acts 5:42**]

People noticed something different about them. [**Acts 4:13**] What caused this profound change that people could see? Let's be sure people can say the same about us!

The Jewish believers changed their Sabbath from Saturday to Sunday.

This is significant. *This was a big deal!* Record what God's Law required according to **Exodus 20:8-10**.

To a God-fearing Jew, the Sabbath to be honored was Saturday. But suddenly a large number of God-fearing Jews who believed they had seen God's Messiah crucified and raised to life again began gathering for worship on Sunday.
Any ideas why?

They celebrated by gathering to worship Him on the day Christ was raised to life ~ Sunday. So do we! We gather in church each Sunday for one purpose ~ *to worship Christ.* For these men and women to abandon the traditional Saturday Sabbath was to put their very souls in jeopardy. They were violating Jewish Law. *They better be right.* But they were convinced of what they saw!

The disciples were willing to die for what they believed

They knew what they KNEW!   They knew what they SAW!

They were willing to die for it. And die, they did:

> James, the brother of John ~ beheaded
> Andrew ~ crucified
> Matthew ~ speared to death
> Bartholomew ~ tortured, then beheaded
> Peter ~ crucified upside down

And on and on the list goes. Every one of the Eleven original disciples suffered and died for the Name of Jesus. So did many others, including Stephen, the first martyr who was stoned to death.

Not one of them changed their stories.

Would you be willing to die for a lie? Would you be willing to die a painful death ~ speared, tortured, crucified, exiled ~ for something that you knew was not true? Neither were they!

What does this sampling of Biblical evidence say to you?

The Resurrection is the crown of the miraculous ministry of Jesus Christ. The Bible powerfully proclaims that His followers saw Jesus walk on water, control nature, multiply bread for thousands not once but twice, cast out demons, exert His authority over Satan, catapult hundreds of powerful soldiers backward at the power of His Name, restore sight to the blind and restore life to the dead! *In the dramatic events of man's salvation, God has the last word in His story!*

Everything that happened those last hours of Christ was in accordance with God's will. It was God's plan of salvation from the foundation of the world. God filled His Word with pictures and visuals of what He was going to do through His Son. Why? Because *His story is the story of our salvation.*

God filled His Word with patterns to teach us about the cross of Jesus because *He wants us to understand*! In this study we've looked at just a few of those patterns, but God has much more in the Bible for us to discover.

That's why studying God's Word is a lifetime pursuit!

Now that you've had a glimpse
As God Sees the Cross,
what do you see *as you see the cross*?

[After jotting down what you see, turn the page and enjoy a "word picture" of what God sees.]

As God Sees The Cross, what does He see?

Glory
Son of God
Garden Promise
Coming Messiah
Animal Skins that protected Adam and Eve
Ram with a Crown of Thorns that saved Isaac
Great High Priest
Morning Sacrifice
Evening Sacrifice
Perfect Sacrifice
The Tabernacle
Burnt Offering
Perfect Blood
Bridegroom
Atonement
His Lamb

JESUS

*_The Works of Josephus, Complete and Unabridged,_
Translated by William Whiston, A.M.,
[Peabody, MA: Hendrickson Publishers, 1987],
The Antiquities of the Jews, 18.3.1ff.

~ ~ ~ ~ ~ ~ ~

Leader's Guide

Welcome to the study of "*As God Sees the Cross.*" It is a wonderful privilege to be the group leader in the study of God's Word! This Leader's Guide has been prepared to assist you with helpful tips and discussion questions to highlight the truths learned. As you lead your group, keep in mind the goal of this study is to present Jesus' salvation work on the cross, and cultivate in others the *desire* to study the Bible. It is my prayer that when the study is completed, no one in your group will ever be the same! Instead, may they have an increased *desire* to spend time in God's Word and make application of its powerful truths in their life.

My first suggestion as you begin is *pray, pray, pray*!! God can use you as an effective leader *only* when you spend time with Him. Always remember ~ *God is our Teacher*. He is asking you to be a facilitator for your group. Your most important role is to encourage them to study and share with each other what God is teaching them.

The guidelines listed here will assure that everyone in your group settles quickly into a study routine and approaches the study with an open heart. I would suggest that these guidelines be explained at your first meeting.

> *Begin by praying, asking God to teach you each time you open His Word.*
>
> *Set aside a special time each day to spend in God's Word.*
>
> *Use only your Bible for your answers.*
>
> *Write down your answers in your book as you study.*
>
> *Complete the lesson each week.*
>
> *When you finish each lesson, ask God to help you memorize the verse that made the strongest impression on you. Write the verse on a card and place it where you will see it often, i.e. your refrigerator, bathroom mirror, or dashboard.*

You may want to share with them this verse taken from Isaiah 40:8:
"*The grass withers and the flowers fall,
but the Word of our God stands forever."*

Encourage your group members that the truths they are learning in the Bible will endure in their lives forever. Studying the powerful Word of God deepens our relationship with Him and changes lives. Challenge your group to *choose to hear from God.* Embark on this adventure by asking yourself: "How do I want my heart to respond to God's teaching?"

Begin each weekly session with prayer. Ask God to teach every member in the group personally through His Word, that each heart will be open to hear His voice, and that everyone will feel comfortable to share some of what God has taught them with the group. If you are nervous about praying with your group, you might want to write your prayer on a card beforehand.

Invite each member of your group to participate. In every lesson there will be questions with answers taken directly from Scripture; these are wonderful chances for the hesitant ones in your group to plunge in and share an answer! There will also be thought provoking questions asking "Why do you think ..." which will lead your group into wonderful discussion. Encourage several people to share their answers on these questions, and try to hear the male and female perspective if you have a mixed group. God teaches us so much from each other.

If there is a particular scripture that was special to you in your preparation time as the group leader, or a scripture that the reader is asked to refer to several times when doing their lesson, it is helpful to have the group look up that scripture together as you read it aloud. You cannot read God's Word too many times!

At the end of each section, the reader is given space to journal what they have learned. *This is so important.* Encourage your group to share some or all of the thoughts recorded on their lists. Keeping a journal record will remind us of the new truths learned and the incredible detail we are seeing in God's Word.

On the pages that follow you will be given the goal for every lesson. As you lead your group each week, make sure that the members understand this truth. You will also be given several application questions for each lesson. These questions will lead your group into discussion. These questions can be used throughout the lesson as you go over your answers, or at the end of the lesson. You will quickly learn to know your group ~ follow their lead on introducing discussion questions. Persuade every member of your group to participate.

It is exciting to hear others share what God is doing in their life now, and to learn to look back and *appreciate that God has been working in their life all along*!

Try to save the last few moments of your time together to allow for any questions. People are often hesitant to interrupt the discussion time, but will appreciate the chance to ask a question at the end.

Finally, and probably most important, *enjoy being the group leader*. Your warmth and enthusiasm will touch the life of every person in your group. It is pure joy to study God's Word. I'm so glad He chose you to lead this group for Him!

Preparing for Passover

Goal: To understand the significance of the Passover meal to the Jewish people. This helps us understand why God chose to have His Passover Lamb triumphantly enter Jerusalem on Lamb Selection Day, the very day God instructed the Jewish families to choose their Passover lamb.

Application Questions:

God required the Jews to look back on Passover and see His mighty Hand in every detail. Can you look back to a time in your life and *now* see that God's mighty hand *was* in every detail of the situation? After looking back, how will you approach your future situations?

Ask God this week:

> To help you recognize God's hand in the details of your daily life and trust Him.

Many Making Plans

Goal: To see that as the Pharisees and chief priests were busy plotting to kill Jesus, He was obediently following God's plan and making preparations for the Passover. Everything that was happening to Jesus was in accordance with God's perfect plan.

Application Questions:

Has there been a time in your life when you had to trust that God's perfect plan was being carried out? What did you learn about trust? Could others see by your response that your faith was in the Lord, not in your circumstances?

Ask God this week:

> To help you see that nothing happens in your life that doesn't pass through God's sovereign Hand first.

An Intimate Proposal

Goal: To understand that Jesus demonstrated the true heart of a servant by washing the disciples' feet.

Application Questions:

How has God called you to be a servant for Him, but you have been hesitant to obey? Why do you think you chose not to respond? *Remember:* As we humbly serve others, we are serving the Lord.

Judas chose to betray Jesus. When have you betrayed Jesus by not standing up or speaking out when you should have? What choices will you make differently?

Ask God this week:

> To open your eyes for opportunities to humbly serve Him.

The Cup of Salvation

Goal: To understand that we are the spiritual bride of Christ.

Application Questions:

A bride will tell anyone who will listen how wonderful her bridegroom is; we should be doing the same thing! What keeps you from initiating conversations about Jesus, or sharing with others what you are learning about your Bridegroom?

How can you become more comfortable to share your faith with others? That's how the Gospel is spread ~ one voice at a time!

Ask God this week:

> To bring someone into your path who needs to hear about Jesus, and give you boldness to tell them how wonderful your Bridegroom is!

Fickle Vow, Faithful Vow

Goal: To understand that Jesus faced His fear and agony in the Garden of Gethsemane, and chose to obey God's will.

Application Questions:

Describe a time when you prayed that God would deliver you from a trial you were experiencing, and God's response.

How did God strengthen your faith and stretch your obedience through that trial? Did God prove faithful?

Ask God this week:

> To help you to desire His Will more than your own, and give you strength to trust Him in this week's trials.

Unwelcome Garden Guests

Goal: To see that Jesus was in complete control of all that was happening. He showed a glimpse of His Majesty as the *Great I AM* ~ then willingly submitted to His arrest.

Application Questions:

Describe an event in your life when you may have felt Jesus wasn't aware of what you were going through. When did He make Himself known in your situation?

What does His Name ~ *I AM* ~ reveal to you about God's nature and character?

Ask God this week:

> To give you a new appreciation for the privilege of asking in prayer in the Name of Jesus.

Forsaking Law and Lord

Goal: To see the hypocrisy in the trials as the Jewish leaders broke every rule in order to crucify Jesus.

Application Questions:

What examples of hypocrisy do you see today in our society, in our leaders, or in our churches?

When do others hear you speak of love for Jesus, and then see you act in a manner that is inconsistent with your words? How are you guilty of *"talking the talk but not walking the walk?"*

Ask God this week:

> To show you any ways you may be acting hypocritical in your Christian walk.

No Fault Found in Him

Goal: To see that Jesus answered clearly for everyone to hear that He is the King of the Jews ~ but the people foolishly chose to follow their religious leaders instead.

Application Questions:

When we "have in mind the things of men, not the things of God," things won't always make sense to us. Is there something going on in your life right now that doesn't make sense in your human eyes?

Can you see circumstances in your life where others may respond, "what a coincidence" ~ but you know that it was a "God-incidence?"

Ask God this week:

> To give you spiritual eyes to see the times in your day when God is intervening ~ your *"God-incidences."*

The Promise of The Cross

Goal: God's promise of the cross reveals the desire of our holy God to come back down to His children and restore fellowship with them.

Application Questions:

Personal holiness is so important to the Lord. Are there areas in your life that you need to surrender to God's standard of holiness?

Can you identify reasons that keep you from allowing God to "come down" to fellowship with you?

Ask God this week:

> To show you areas in your life where you are not living in personal holiness.

Walking the Blood Path

Goal: To appreciate that before the foundation of the world, Jesus promised to fulfill the vow of the Lord and *walk the blood path* alone

Application Questions:

The Bible is filled with promises that God is faithful to keep. Share with the group a promise in God's Word that is special to you.

We are not as faithful in keeping our promises. How well do you keep promises? How do you respond when others break theirs?

Ask God this week:

> To remind you to read God's promises back to Him when you pray because it pleases Him when we pray His Word.

The Daily Sacrifice

Goal: To understand that Jesus was the perfect sacrifice. On that cross God poured out His wrath against sin; then turned His back as the Precious Lamb of God "took away the sin of the world" on that altar.

Application Questions:

As you reflect on the cross, how do you see your sin differently? If you were the only person on earth, God would still require that Jesus die on the cross for your sin. How do you respond to such a sacrifice?

Ask God this week:

> To give you a renewed determination to turn from sin, and a heart of gratitude for the forgiveness available to you.

The Cries from the Cross

Goal: In the seven cries from the cross, the words of Jesus are examples of forgiveness, perfect love, obedience, and the victory that is ours in Christ Jesus.

Application Questions:

How did you react the last time someone's words hurt you? What have you learned about forgiveness from Jesus' example?

Have your words hurt someone; do you need to seek forgiveness?

Ask God this week:

> To make you sensitive to the impact your words may have on others, and give you the desire to seek forgiveness from anyone you have hurt with your words.

The Earth Shook

Goal: To understand that when Christ died, God reached down and ripped the curtain in the temple from top to bottom. The barrier separating God and man has been broken.

Application Questions:

God removed the barrier; yet we foolishly allow "things" to put the barrier back. What are the priorities in your life ~ your barriers ~ that have come before God and need to be removed?

We are sometimes so wrapped up in ourselves that WE become the barrier; are there any changes you may need to make?

Ask God this week:

> To reveal the barriers that need to be removed and allow God to become your first priority.

A Sign in a Secure Tomb

Goal: To "see," as Mary Magdalene saw, that the place where Jesus' body lay became the true Mercy Seat on earth.

Application Questions:

Mercy is such a sweet word ~ God's love spared us from the punishment we justly deserved. How can we guard against taking advantage of God's mercy and becoming cavalier about our sin?

Peter went away from that tomb wondering to himself because Jesus left a sign to remind us He is coming back. How should that wonderful assurance impact your life?

Ask God this week:

> To give you wisdom to live each day as you would if you knew Jesus was returning today!

Atonement

Goal: To understand that the Son presented His perfect blood to the Father and made peace for us. We are *at one* with God again *only* by the blood of Jesus.

Application Questions:

Many people think they can "work" their way to heaven by their own goodness. If you stood at heaven's gate and God asked you why He should let you into His heaven, what would your response be?

How will you now share with anyone trying in vain to "work" their way to heaven, the truth that *Jesus is the only way*?

Ask God this week:

To give you the courage to share the truth that you have learned ~ it is the truth that saves lives!

Note to Leader: This is an ideal opportunity to follow up on the prayer included in this lesson. Begin by asking if each one in your group is sure beyond doubt that their eternity will be spent in heaven because they know Jesus as Savior. If any in the group prayed to receive Jesus as a result of this lesson, encourage them to share their decision if they feel comfortable doing so. They may prefer to share privately with you. Others in the group may have questions; be available to talk individually with them.

Powerful Evidence

Goal: The Bible contains powerful evidence that Jesus is alive.

Application Questions:

When a person asks Jesus to be their Savior, their life changes; sometimes dramatically!   What evidence do others see that Jesus is now Lord of your life? Evidence that can be seen causes others to "want what you have."

What would you say to someone who notices "what you have" in your life and asks how to get it? Your *life* may be the only Bible some people ever read.

Ask God this week:

> To display in your life evidence for everyone to see that Jesus is your Lord and Savior.

~~~~~

You have come to the end of an incredible experience. God chose you to lead your group in an adventure to see the cross *"As God Sees the Cross."*   They have been blessed by your faithfulness and lives have been changed.   Most importantly, God has been honored by your obedience.

May this be just the beginning of your journey into God's Word. It is a lifetime adventure!